Guitar Tablature Explained

The Musical Staff shows notes and rests, and is divided by lines into measures. Notes are named after the first seven letters of the alphabet.

The Tablature Staff graphically represents the guitar fingerboard. Each horizontal line represents a string, and each number represents a fret.

Special Guitar Notation

Half-Step Bend: Strike the note and bend up a one half-step.

Whole-Step Bend: Strike the note and bend up one whole step.

Grace Note Bend: Strike the note and bend as indicated. Play the first note as quickly as possible.

Quarter-Tone Bend: Strike the note and bend up a quarter step.

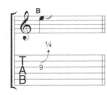

Hammeron: Strike the string normally to play the first note. Bring down a left-hand finger at the indicated fret to sound the second note.

Pulloff: Place left-hand fingers on both notes to be sounded. Strike the string normally to play the first note. Remove the higher left-hand finger from the string, to sound the second note.

Bend and Release: Strike the note and bend up as indicated, then release back to the original note.

Legato Slide (Gliss): Strike the first note and then slide the same fret-hand finger up or down to the second note. The second note is not struck.

Shift Slide (Gliss & Restrike): Same as legato slide, except the second note is struck.

Contents

Playing Techniques

Check Your Hand Positions 6
The Guide Finger 8
The Capo: Transposing Made Easy 10
The Capo: Better Fingerpicking 12
The Capo: A Fuller Sound 13
The Art of Fingering 14
Pick and Fingers 16
More Tones from Your Electric Guitar 18
Violin Tone 20

Gear

Wah-Wah Effect 21
Using a Power Soak 22
Using Two Distortion Circuits 23

Tricks for Soloists

How to Play Lead 24
Playing Lead with Open Strings 26
Riffing with Open Strings 27
Fingering a Lead Run 28
Play Lead Without Learning Scales 29
Getting the Most from a Lead Lick 30
Great Solos with No Effort 32
Play Blues Lead the Easy Way 34

THE LITTLE BOOK OF
TIPS & TRICKS FOR GUITAR

The complete guide to techniques, soloing, rhythm, and styles.

Amsco Publications
New York/London/Paris/Sydney/Copenhagen/Madrid

Cover photography by Randall Wallace

This book Copyright © 2000 by Amsco Publications,
A Division of Music Sales Corporation, New York

All rights reserved. No part of this book may be
reproduced in any form or by any electronic or mechanical means,
including information storage and retrieval systems,
without permission in writing from the publisher.

Order No. AM 954767
US International Standard Book Number: 0.8256.1808.8
UK International Standard Book Number: 0.7119.7821.2

Exclusive Distributors:
Music Sales Corporation
257 Park Avenue South, New York, NY 10010 USA
Music Sales Limited
8/9 Frith Street, London W1D 3JB England
Music Sales Pty. Limited
120 Rothschild Street, Rosebery, Sydney, NSW 2018, Australia

Printed in the United States of America by
Vicks Lithograph and Printing Corporation

Rhythm Tips

Dropped D Tuning for Rockers 36
Dropped D Tuning for Fingerpickers 38
Going Up with D 40
Going Up with C 41
Slide Guitar in Standard Tuning 42
Power Chords 43
More Power Chords 44
Power Fourths 45
Perfect Bar Chords 46
Two More Altered Tunings 48

Style Ideas

Two Rock and Roll Rhythm Figures 50
Add Some Eastern Flavor 52
Alternate Picking for Indie Guitar 53
Better Tone for Fingerstyle Guitar 54
Hendrix-Style Rhythm Lick 55
Hendrix-Style Broken Chords 56
How to Start a Blues Solo 58
Knopfler-Style Rhythm 59
More Blues Licks 60
Quick-Change Blues 61
Writing Songs 62

Check Your Hand Positions

Playing the guitar is easy when you use good right and left hand positioning.

The Thumb

Place your left hand on the fretboard. Make sure that your thumb remains vertical and behind the first finger and second finger.

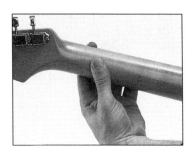

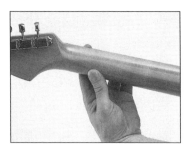

The Palm

Don't let your left palm touch the neck of the guitar. Such a position will compromise the movement of your fingers. Allow your thumb to retain its natural curve.

Barring

When you play a bar chord, lower the thumb so that its end is lower than the top of the fingerboard.

Playing Techniques

String Bending

When bending strings, curl the thumb slightly over the top of the neck to get more leverage.

Strumming

When strumming, the main movement comes from the arm rather than the hand (although the hand can make small accentuating movements). There's no need to sweep too far below the strings or rise too far above them.

Picking

When picking, the movement comes from the hand, primarily the thumb and first finger (holding the pick). The forearm should not move back and forth. You may find it helps to rest your forearm on the body of the guitar to stabilize your hand.

The Guide Finger

One useful thing to be aware of when you play is the concept of the *guide finger*. This is a finger that stays on a single string during a sequence of chords. A guide finger makes it easy to play and remember chord changes.

In this first example you'll find a sequence of sixths (notes an interval of a sixth apart). These intervals are often used as decorative lead figures. Notice that the second finger acts as a guide, always on the lowest note of each pair, while the upper note is played either with the first or third finger.

In the second example there is a sequence of thirds. In bars 1 and 2 the second finger acts as a guide. In bars 3 and 4, it's the first finger.

Playing Techniques

When you are working out a chord progression, check if there is a finger that doesn't need to move, or a finger that only needs to move up or down one string.

Try the following chord sequence.

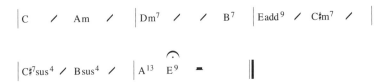

Notice how the first finger doesn't move until B7, how the third finger stays still as you go from Dm7 to B7, how the second and fourth fingers stay still going to Eadd9, how the third finger is a guide up the fourth string as you change to C#m7, and so on.

Each chord is connected to the next either by a finger that doesn't move or one that moves up or down a string.

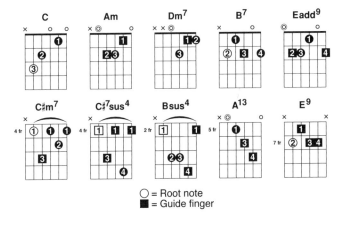

The Capo: Transposing Made Easy

The capo is a very useful accessory. Imagine if you had to play the following chord progression.

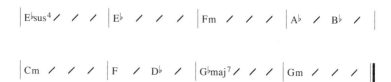

Every one of these chords is barred. Such a progression can become very tiring for the fretting hand. It is also difficult to add embellishments to the sequence because almost every chord requires that all the fingers be used. A capo solves the problem neatly.

By placing a capo at the first fret, all the chords can be played one half-step lower. Most of these now become a lot easier to play. The chord in parentheses is the actual pitch—the chord name is the familiar open position shape.

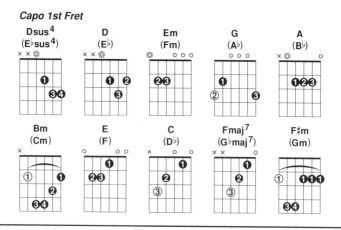

Here's another example of a chord sequence with several barred chords.

A capo

| C# / / / | C#maj^7 / / / | C#^{7} / / / | D#m / F# / |

| G#^{7} / / / | A#m^{11} / / / | D#^{7} / / / | E#m / B / ‖

Without a capo this would be very tiring for the fretting hand. With a capo at the fourth fret, it becomes much easier to play.

The chord boxes give the chord name first (as if in open position) and the actual pitch second. The capo is at the fourth fret. Four frets is two whole steps, so each chord is represented by the chord two tones below it.

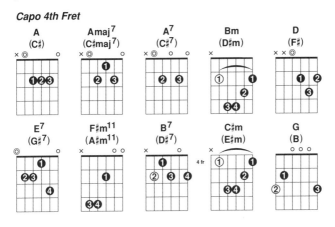

The Capo: Better Fingerpicking

Another consequence of a high capo is that it becomes possible to finger combinations of notes that would be impossible lower down. This arises because the frets are closer together.

This short fingerpicked piece has many note clusters that are only playable because the capo is at the seventh fret. Listen to the chiming effect caused by notes that are either very close (as in bars 2 and 7) or at the same pitch (bar 3).

Note that the TAB numbers refer to the capoed guitar, so that the first note is two frets above the capo, which is actually the 9th fret of the guitar. For the purposes of this example, the standard notation shows the notes at pitch.

The Capo: A Fuller Sound

A capo can be used to produce different tone qualities. If the capo is placed quite high on the neck, the sound becomes higher and brighter.

A capo can also be used to achieve a fuller sound in a guitar duo. Imagine you're playing a song with this chord progression.

| E / / / | C#m / / / | A / F#m / | B^7 / / / ||

The first five chord boxes show how you could play this sequence with the usual chord forms.

Guitar 1 - Open Position

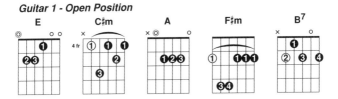

The second five chord boxes show the same chords played on another guitar with a capo at the seventh position. The chord form comes first, the actual pitch is shown in parentheses.

Guitar 2 - Capo seventh Fret

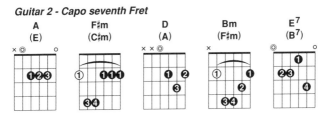

When both guitars are playing the sound is fuller because Guitar 2's chords are pitched higher, creating a twelve-string effect.

The Art of Fingering

Good fingering is the art of knowing which fingers should hold down notes and chords. If you get your fingering right, everything will be easier to play.

Sometimes it's a good idea to change the fingering of a common chord in order to make a change easier. Check out these five examples to find out how strategic fingering can make certain chord changes easier.

Refingering this G chord makes it easier to change to C because your second and third fingers only need to move across one string from the bottom two strings.

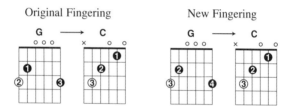

By refingering this G chord, your fourth finger can remain in place as you change to Dsus4.

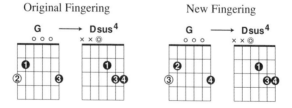

Here, by changing the E chord fingering, it becomes easier to move up five frets and add a first finger bar to form the A chord.

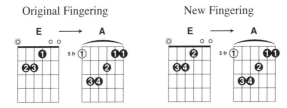

Here's another bar chord that can be made much easier by altering the fingering slightly. With the new fingering all you have to do is move the shape to its new position and add the bar.

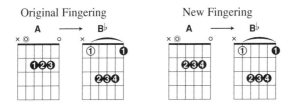

This bass note change can be simplified by refingering the Dm chord to leave your third finger free to play the C on the D string.

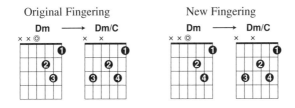

Pick and Fingers

One of the most useful picking techniques is the ability to use a pick and fingers together. For this reason, the pick should always be held between the thumb and the first finger.

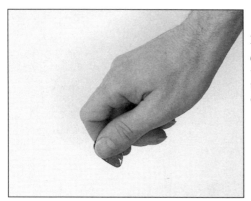

Pick Grip

Grip the pick firmly with the flat part of the thumb against the side of the first finger.

Pick Position

Here the pick is being held in the normal way, but the other fingers are also being used to pick the strings.

Playing Techniques

The next example gives you an opportunity to try this technique. The pick always hits the lowest note with a downstroke. The second and third fingers pluck the other notes. Once you get the hang of it, gradually speed up to achieve an almost classical effect.

Pay attention to the picking pattern in this example. The letter *p* refers to the pick, which should be held in the usual way, while using the *m* and *a* fingers to pluck the other strings.

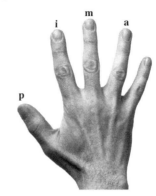

R.H. p m a p m a p m a p m a (etc.)

The pick and fingers technique creates a fingerpicking effect but leaves you with the option of moving into single-note lead soloing or heavy strumming.

More Tones from Your Electric Guitar

Electric guitarists tend to associate the number of pickups or pickup selections they have with the number of tones they can get from their instrument. Actually, you can always get more tones from your guitar without buying any more equipment.

Pickup Selection

Select any pickup on your guitar and make sure you have a clean sound and enough volume to hear clearly.

— **Volume control**

— **Pickup selector**

— **Tone controls**

Your Usual Tone

Strike the G string wherever your picking hand normally hits it. That establishes your usual tone.

Playing Techniques

Changing the Tone

Now strike the string over the very end of the fingerboard. It's a different tone even though you're on the same pickup.

Keep striking the G string, but gradually move your hand toward the bridge.

Experimenting

As you do this, you will hear the tone changing continually and becoming thinner, more brittle and more trebly as you approach the bridge.

Change pickups and repeat the process. You will hear different tones. You can use these tones in your playing simply by moving your picking hand a few inches.

Don't forget that the volume and tone knobs on your guitar will also have an effect on tone. For a jazzy underwater sound, try the neck pickup with the tone turned all the way down.

Violin Tone

There's one great sound effect you can get from an electric guitar at no extra expense: violin tone. To do it, you need a fair amount of volume from the amplifier.

Begin by turning the volume off on the guitar itself. Then curl your little finger around the volume knob. Strike the string and turn the volume up with your finger. If you do it correctly, the note you have struck will increase in volume. Guitar notes usually decay from loud to soft. If the timing is good you won't hear the actual strike of the string. The string should already be vibrating when the volume is still off. As you turn the knob a note will be heard.

Turning the knob and striking strings at the same time can be tricky. A lot depends on the layout of your guitar and how far the volume knobs are from the strings. If you're using a distorted sound, try hammering-on the notes with your fretting hand.

Violin-tone also sounds great with echo. You can buy a volume pedal which allows you to create this effect with your foot.

Violining

This technique is easier on a *Strat* than a *Les Paul* due to the position of the volume control.

Listen to "Xanadu" by Rush, and "Cathedral" by Eddie Van Halen for classic examples of this technique.

Wah-Wah Effect

Wah-wah pedals were first used in the late 1960s and remain popular with electric guitarists today.

Different pedals have different actions. When the pedal is open, the treble frequencies are cut giving a muted sound. When the pedal is shut, the treble frequencies are boosted. You can set the pedal to either of these positions and simply leave it there.

For the wah sound itself there is a critical angle (usually about half-way down) at which the audible change in the note is at its maximum. To play a wah-wah successfully you need to "ride" that point the way a surfer rides a wave. You don't need to pump the pedal up and down. Just a subtle touch back and forth on that "crossover" point will do the trick.

To get the classic *Shaft* soundtrack sound, mute all the strings strum sixteenth notes (four times each beat), and slowly moving the pedal up and down. Another classic effect is to play a lead phrase with a few repeated notes and gradually move the pedal from open to shut and back again. The changing frequencies will be more noticeable because the notes remain the same.

Wah-Wah Pedal

The much loved "Crybaby" wah-wah pedal. Never leave the house without one!

Using a Power Soak

The trouble with big tube amps is that by the time you've turned them up far enough to get a rich distortion from the tubes the volume level is unmanageable and everyone else in the band is complaining.

The *power soak* is a gadget which will help you with this. It's a circuit that acts as an attenuator, absorbing some of the amp's power before it reaches the speakers. It plugs in between the amp head and the speaker cabinet and usually has several settings, depending on how much energy you want to absorb. The power soak gives you instant tube distortion with no artificial ingredients.

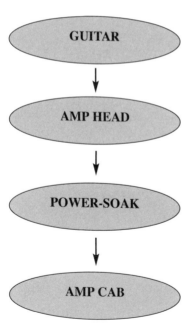

Once you have your amp set up with the power soak as shown here, you can alter the sound of your guitar quite drastically by altering its volume control. Turn the volume right down for a punchy, clean sound (ideal for rhythm playing), or turn it right up for a screaming, distorted solo.

You'll also find that this set-up will make your guitar much more responsive to subtleties of touch and articulation. The playing of Jimi Hendrix provides a classic example.

Using Two Distortion Circuits

Rock players often find that they need two distortion sounds—one for rhythm and the other for lead. The problem with trying to use one distortion sound is that if it is thick enough for single note lead playing, it makes chords sound mushy—and if it is clear enough for the chords it doesn't have enough sustain and penetration for lead.

One way out of this is to use the volume knob on the guitar. Turn this up to full volume. Now adjust your distortion circuit (in a pedal or in the amp) until you get the type of distortion you want for lead (with the volume level you need for the solo). Now turn the volume knob down until you find a level that's right for rhythm. Some of the distortion will thin out because the pickup isn't being driven flat-out.

Another solution is to use two distortion/overdrive circuits. Make sure the volume on your guitar is on full. Then set the first distortion to give you a good rhythm sound. Now set the second to add a little extra distortion and more volume by turning up its own volume control. Then when you want to solo you can just turn on the second distortion circuit. The first circuit could be in the amp itself; the second could be a pedal. Pedals labelled as "overdrive" rather than out-and-out distortions are sufficient for this purpose.

More Gadgets

Here are two common effects pedals you could use to achieve the above effect—a Boss OD-1 Overdrive and an Ibanez Tube Screamer.

How to Play Lead

So, you'd like to start playing solos, but don't know how to go about it? Here's a quick way to get you started.

Below are three A pentatonic minor scales. Each includes five notes: A C D E G. The first scale is situated at the fifth fret. The second is basically the same, except there is a little extension at the top which takes you a few frets higher. The third scale is one octave higher than the first. These patterns cover quite a bit of the fretboard and provide ample material for a solo.

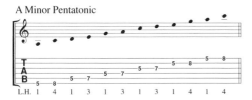

A Pentatonic Minor

This is the basic moveable pattern, and doesn't use finger extensions or hand position changes.

With Extension

You'll find yourself playing some different phrases with this pattern, which shifts position to reach the twelfth fret.

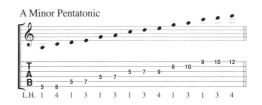

An Octave Higher

Don't be put off by the high numbers—the frets are closer together at the top of neck so there's less stress on your fingers.

Try using these scales over a twelve-bar sequence in A or A minor. You can also use them for anything in the key of C major. That's because every pentatonic minor scale is also the pentatonic major of the note three half-steps higher (A to C = three half-steps). It is the chord sequence that will determine whether the scale is heard as A pentatonic minor or C pentatonic major.

Playing Lead with Open Strings

Playing single-note lead runs can sometimes sound a bit thin, especially in a three-piece band. Here's a way of making a bigger sound as you solo by using an open string.

If you're playing in a major or minor key where E, B, or G is an important note (*i.e.,* the root or the fifth of the scale), you can play lead phrases up and down an adjacent string while hitting the open string at the same time.

This example shows an ascending lead melody in E major with an open-string E sounding above it all the way through. Just add a touch of distortion and echo for a big sound.

String Clearance

Make sure you lift up onto the tips of your fingers to ensure the top E (first) string rings out clearly while you fret notes on the B (second) string.

Tricks for Soloists

Riffing with Open Strings

Open bass strings can also be used to make a riff sound bigger. When they occur as bass notes below a moving line they're called *pedal tones*. On the guitar, E, A, and D are possible pedal notes.

In this example, a riff is moving up and down the G string on a Dorian scale (D E F G A B C D). Underneath, the D string is sounding throughout. The effect is surprisingly full. Again, effects such as distortion, chorus, and/or echo will make it even fuller.

The Dorian Mode

Much used by Carlos Santana, this mode is basically a natural minor with a sharped 6th.

Fingering a Lead Run

It's not just chord sequences that benefit from good fingering. Obviously, fingering becomes crucial if you're trying to play at speed.

One good approach to fingering single-note runs is to organize everything into a four-fret box in which each finger is dedicated to one fret. With these positions, playing fast lead runs becomes a lot easier. The Roman numeral over the staff indicates the starting fret (or position).

The example below starts at second position, with each finger working one fret. In bars 5 and 6 the solo changes position several times—but watch what happens to the fingering. Bar 7 extends the box to five because these frets are sufficiently close together to allow the fingers to cover five frets.

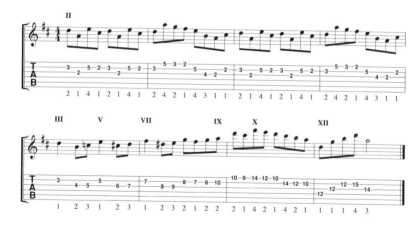

Remember that if a lead run involves bending notes you'll need a different fingering to avoid bending with the weak little finger.

Tricks for Soloists

Play Lead Without Learning Scales

You might think that in order to play lead solos you have to know lots of scales. Here's a trick that will allow you to create some great solos by using phrases based on chords rather than scales.

In this example the first four bars use triads (a *triad* is any chord consisting of three notes). In bars 5 through 8 these are repeated and extended downward. Notice how these figures can incorporate bends and pulloffs.

Because you're outlining the chords themselves, your playing will sound more melodic. This is very different from the standard approach, where you use one scale that will work over an entire chord sequence.

This is the beginning of what jazz musicians would call "playing over the changes," where the soloist adopts a different set of scales and arpeggios for every chord change. This technique can be used effectively in nearly all forms of music.

Getting the Most from a Lead Lick

Here's another useful trick for playing lead licks without learning hundreds of phrases. All you need to do is modify a phrase you already know.

Remember this important rule: The musical value of a lead phrase or note depends upon the harmony that supports it. The practical effect of this is that playing the same phrase over different chords will alter its sound.

Try this two bar phrase over a C chord. Beneath the staff, you'll find an analysis of its harmonic value. The numbers that are circled are the notes of the C major chord. The more circled numbers, the better the lick will sound.

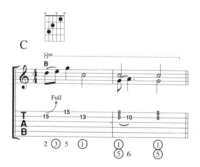

The following five diagrams are an analysis of the same notes played against the other chords in the key of C major: Dm, Em, F, G, and Am. The notes stay the same but their harmonic values change to create totally different sounds.

Tricks for Soloists

Great Solos with No Effort

Check out the following chord progression in the key of C major.

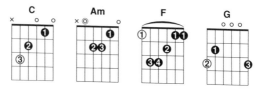

Most guitarists would automatically use a C major pentatonic or A minor pentatonic scale to solo over this progression.

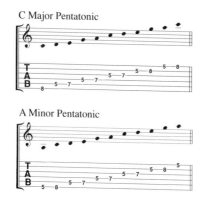

An E minor pentatonic scale also works well with this progression. Here's the scale, followed by a few bars of lead solo.

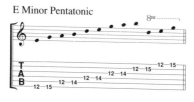

Tricks for Soloists

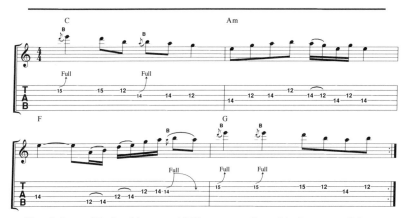

How is it possible for this to work? You can see from this that none of the notes from C pentatonic and E pentatonic minor fall outside those found in the full C major scale—and therefore they won't clash.

C major scale: C D E F G A B C
C major pentatonic: C D E G A
E minor pentatonic: E G A B D

However, these two pentatonic scales do differ slightly. The diagram below shows the notes common to both scales (arrowed) and the notes that differ (circled).

In E minor pentatonic the key note (C) is missing. This gives the scale an unusual quality, especially if you play the entire solo using it rather than combining it with a C scale. To do this in other major keys, simply use the pentatonic minor which is two whole-steps above your key note.

Play Blues Lead the Easy Way

Most inexperienced blues players have a tendency to overuse the pentatonic minor. Here's an easy trick for instantly transforming the sound of your blues solos.

You should recognize the first two scales: A pentatonic minor followed by an extension box around the eighth fret.

The extension box is the upper part of the next position of the A pentatonic minor, and many players find this fragment of it invaluable for extending the range of the basic scale.

A Pentatonic Minor

This is the first blues scale many people learn, but it's a lot more versatile than you might realize.

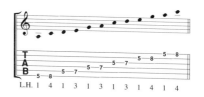

Extension Box

Try this useful extension to the A pentatonic minor for a little more range and many more options.

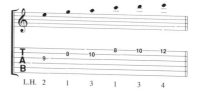

Imagine you're playing a twelve-bar blues in A. If you move these scale patterns down three frets they automatically convert into the major pentatonic for the same key—so you don't have to learn a new pattern!

This works anywhere on the neck above the first couple of frets. Moving down three frets creates a radical change in tone. The pentatonic major sounds much more upbeat.

Mixing the two scales will make your blues solos more interesting.

A Pentatonic Major

You can use this major scale as a substitute for the pentatonic minor.

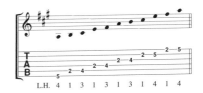

Extension Box

For added range, use this A pentatonic minor extension.

Remember, in a major key you can play pentatonic minor and major scales. In a minor key, you can't play any major scales.

Dropped D Tuning for Rockers

One area of guitar-playing that has become increasingly popular is the use of altered and open tunings. These tunings put new sounds within the reach of the guitarist and can stimulate creativity.

Dropped D tuning is both popular and easy to use. For this tuning, lower the bottom E down to D. You can check if it's in tune either by comparing it with the open fourth string (which is a D one octave higher) or by holding down the seventh fret on the bottom string and checking that it is the same as the open A.

Hard rock and grunge players like this tuning because it creates a low, easily fingered power-chord.

Tuning Guide						
String Number	6	5	4	3	2	1
Standard Tuning	E	A	D	G	B	E
Dropped D Tuning	**D**	**A**	**D**	**G**	**B**	**E**
Alteration Necessary	-2	-	-	-	-	-
Interval Between Strings (in half-steps/frets)	7	5	5	4	5	

When you try playing this example, remember you can now play the bottom strings on the D chord.

Dropped D Tuning for Fingerpickers

Dropped D tuning is also popular with fingerpickers. In folk styles, the tuning offers an octave of two open-string D notes (the sixth and fourth strings) which can be played by the thumb in an alternating bass movement.

As these notes are open strings, the fretting hand is free to go where it wishes and play a melody.

Tuning Guide						
String Number	6	5	4	3	2	1
Standard Tuning	E	A	D	G	B	E
Dropped D Tuning	**D**	**A**	**D**	**G**	**B**	**E**
Alteration Necessary	-2	-	-	-	-	-
Interval Between Strings (in half-steps/frets)	7	5	5	4	5	

Rhythm Tips

Play this piece to get a taste for this folk bass-and-melody style.

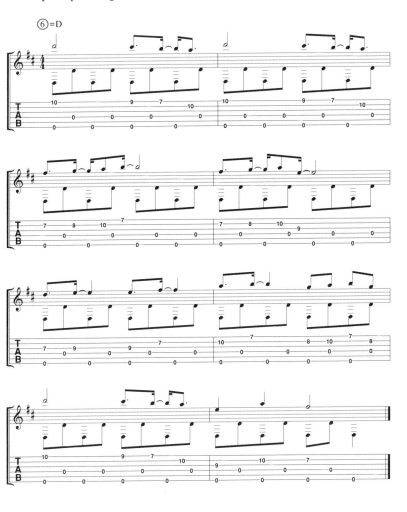

Going Up with D

It's fun to experiment with chord forms on the guitar. All you need to do is pick a shape, move it up the neck, and find out where it sounds best.

The D chord is a good form to experiment with. The eight chord boxes below show you how to play a series of major triads while the D note sounds underneath.

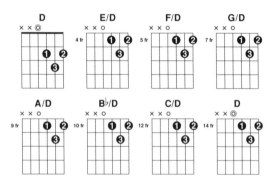

D Major Chord

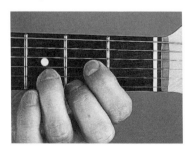

Slash chords, such as the F/D chord shown above, can be named in different ways. F/D literally means an F chord with a D note in the bass, but this could also be called Dm7, as it contains the notes D, F, A, and C.

Going Up with C

Here's another example of how a chord form changes as it moves up the fretboard. Start with an ordinary C chord. Note that it has three fretted notes (C, E, and C) and two open strings (G and E). As the shape moves up the neck the fretted notes always maintain the same relation to each other, but the open strings remain G and E. These open notes form new relationships with each new chord.

In the chord boxes below, you'll notice that a finger is sometimes added on the top string to make the chord more effective.

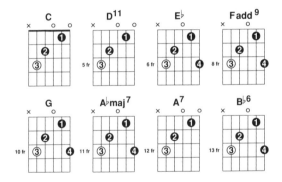

C Major Shape

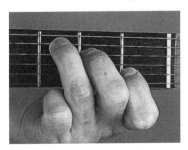

Slide Guitar in Standard Tuning

Slide or bottleneck guitar is often associated with open tunings such as G (D G D G B D) or A (E A E A C♯ E). However, what happens if you need to play some bottleneck chords in standard tuning? Here's a tip.

To get a major or minor chord, you only need three notes. This is called a *triad*. The top three strings make a minor triad (EBG)—E minor chord with the root note at the top. The second, third, and fourth strings make a major triad (BGD)—a G major chord with the root note in the middle.

By using the right fret positions and combination of strings you can play these major and minor triads along with any chord progression in any key. The chord boxes below show some positions for the seven most likely chords for a song in C major.

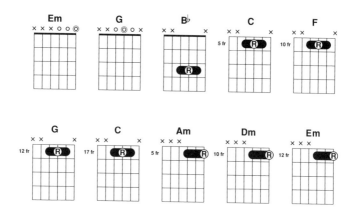

The *R* in each slide guitar chord indicates its root note.

Power Chords

To get a heavier, tougher guitar sound when playing a chord sequence, try using power chords. The correct term for these is *fifths*. These are written C5, F5, G5, and so on.

The five chord boxes below show some fifths with just two notes. Fifth chords are neither major nor minor. That means you can play them underneath a chord progression regardless of whether it is in a major or minor key.

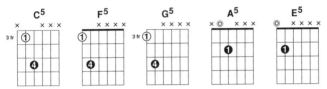

The next five chord boxes feature a few more strings. Notice that you haven't added any new notes—it's still only two in each chord, but these are doubled or tripled.

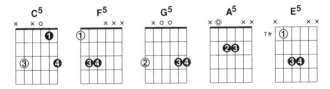

Bar Alternative

You can play the upper notes of the moveable power chords (such as E5 and F5 in the second chord group above) with a partial bar. Just lay the third or fourth finger flat across both strings.

More Power Chords

Since there are only two notes in a power chord, these can be played in many different positions on the fretboard.

The chord boxes below show ten different ways of playing an A5 chord.

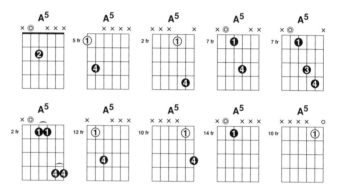

Many variations are possible for other power chords, especially those that include open strings. Try to find as many E5 and D5 forms as you can on the fretboard. Here are a few to start you off.

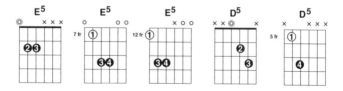

Power Fourths

If you turn a fifth upside-down you get a *fourth:* CG becomes GC. Fourths are another useful tool to use when playing rock guitar. They don't work well for chugging rhythm figures, but they are great in riffs and lead guitar solos.

Here are some examples.

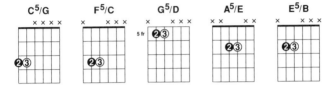

You may find it easier to play these using a first-finger bar. Try the examples below.

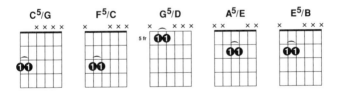

Although these chords are called fourths we write them as slash chords to avoid confusing them with another type of chord called a suspended fourth. C5/G indicates a C power chord with the G in the bass.

Perfect Bar Chords

One of the more difficult techniques for the guitarist is the bar chord. A bar chord involves holding more than one string down with the same finger—often the first finger, but sometimes the third or fourth.

To start with, most players find it hard holding down more than one string with the same finger. You will need to build some strength in your fretting hand, but here are some other solutions.

String Action

Make sure that the action (the height of the strings above the fretboard) on your guitar is low. This will instantly help you hold down more strings. If it is too high, take it into a guitar shop to have it adjusted.

Lighter Strings

Try changing to a lighter string gauge. Lighter strings need less tension and are easier to press down.

Thumb Position

Make sure that the thumb of your fretting hand remains vertical, but drops below the neck to enable the fingers to open out and stretch. If you are not using your second finger in the chord, try putting it on top of the first finger making the bar to increase pressure on the strings.

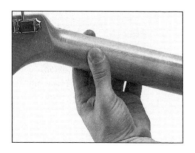

Bar Technique

When you bar with your first finger, roll the finger very slightly toward the headstock end of the neck. By exerting more pressure with that edge of the finger, you can make a better contact with the string.

Don't always practice bar chords at the first fret. String tension is usually high there because the string is right next to the nut. Try moving a few frets up instead.

These chords will help you gradually develop your barring technique. Try playing them at higher frets until you have built up strength in your fretting hand. Then move them back down to the bottom of the neck.

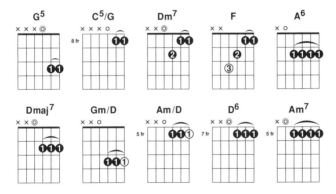

Two More Altered Tunings

Experimenting with altered tunings can be a little confusing. If you change as few as two strings, the layout of notes on the fretboard can become unrecognizable. Fortunately you don't have to go that far.

Start by changing one string and experimenting with the new chords you discover.

We've seen what happens when you take the bottom E string down to D. now try the reverse and take the top E string down to D. To check the new tuning, either compare the top string with the fourth (D), or compare it with the D that's at the third fret on the B string.

Here are some chords in this new tuning. Notice that chord boxes 6 through 10 contain familiar chord forms that now sound different because one string has been changed.

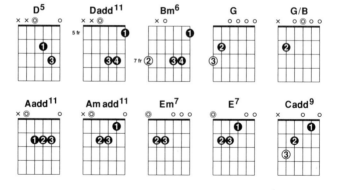

Here's another tuning that features a single string alteration. Take the third string G down a half-step to F♯. You can use the F♯ that's at the fourth fret on the D string as a reference point.

As before, some familiar forms now sound different. Notice the beautifully resonant B/Bm chords. In standard tuning, these would be bar chords, but here they are full of open strings!

This tuning is sometimes called *lute tuning*.

Tuning Guide						
String Number	6	5	4	3	2	1
Standard Tuning	E	A	D	G	B	E
Lute Tuning	E	A	D	F♯	B	E
Alteration Necessary	-	-	-	-1	-	-
Interval Between Strings (in half-steps/frets)	5	5	4	5	5	

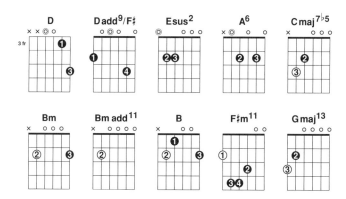

Two Rock and Roll Rhythm Figures

Here's a famous rock and roll rhythm figure, used since the 1950s.

In the first bar, you'll see the E5/E6 riff played down low. Try to strike both notes evenly. This also works if you move it up to the A string and D string.

In the second bar, the riff is played one octave higher. Keep your thumb behind the neck so that your fingers can stretch to finger these notes. In the third bar, the figure is played at the same pitch but one string higher (at the 7th fret.)

Bars 2 and 3 are moveable patterns (they don't use any open strings). You can use these riff patterns for any chord.

If you were playing a twelve-bar blues in the key of A, you could start on the bottom string at fret 5 and play the D and E chords on the fifth string at frets 5 and 7. Alternatively you could start on the fifth string at fret 12 and then move down from there. Try to memorize the shape of these chords.

Style Ideas

This full-bodied rhythm lick makes a great complement to the one on the facing page. Using more notes, it has a fatter sound.

First play an A chord at the second fret using a first finger bar. This is the position for an A6 chord (but you're not going to hit the top string, just the middle four). Bring down your second and third fingers to play a D/A chord, as shown in the diagram. Then lift these two fingers to go back to the barred A chord.

To play this figure with other chords is slightly more tricky. For example, when the riff is moved up to B, the bass note can only be fingered by the little finger reaching onto the bottom string and deadening the fifth string at the same time. This requires practice. If you find it too difficult, just leave the bass note out.

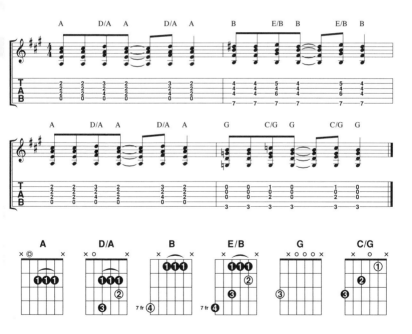

Add Some Eastern Flavor

There are three main types of minor scale: the *natural*, the *harmonic*, and the *melodic*. Of these, the harmonic is the most unusual in sound. This is because it has a gap of three half-steps between the sixth and seventh notes with one half-step before and after.

It is easy to take this part of the scale and exploit it for an Eastern sounding lead line, as this example shows. It sounds even more exotic with the addition of string bends, in the third and fourth bars.

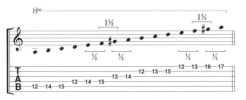

A Harmonic Minor

Watch the stretches between the sixth and seventh notes of the scale; it's this interval that is responsible for the scale's unusual sound. Check out the solo in "Don't Fear the Reaper" by Blue Oyster Cult to hear the harmonic minor scale in action.

Style Ideas

Alternate Picking for Indie Guitar

Indie guitar styles are often chordal-based and feature arpeggios. Sometimes this involves rapid picking of the strings. To do this successfully, it is important to practice alternate picking.

Alternate picking means playing downstrokes and upstrokes with the pick, to make the most of each pick movement. If you've picked a note downward, hit it again on the way back up.

Try the following chord sequence with strict alternate picking: down-up down-up, *etc*. Start off slowly and then gradually speed it up, aim to create a steady sound. Try not to look at the strings as you play.

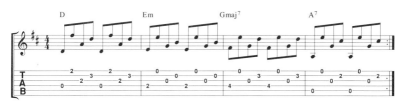

For a typical indie sound, you could try playing this on a twelve-string Rickenbacker—or adding a small amount of chorus and reverb to any electric guitar. Check out the recordings of Johnny Marr (The Smiths), Peter Buck (R.E.M.), and John Squire (Stone Roses) to hear this style in action.

Better Tone for Fingerstyle Guitar

Here's a neat tip for fingerstyle players who like to use their nails. Have you noticed how your picking fingers can catch on the strings, causing you to stumble over some passages?

To help reduce the friction of the nail against the string, get some very fine emery paper. Use it to round off any hard edges so that your nail has a smooth curve from one side to the other.

Then use the paper to bevel the inside edge of the nail (between the nail and the finger). You can achieve this by holding the edge of the nail at an angle to the paper. This puts a slight slope on the inside edge of the nail. When you hit the string, your nail will slide over it smoothly.

The result: less of a feeling that your fingers are catching against the strings and a better tone.

Hendrix-Style Rhythm Lick

The legendary playing of Jimi Hendrix has many facets. Although people often think of him tearing lead lick after lead lick from an amped-up Stratocaster, he was also an innovative rhythm player.

Here's a Hendrix-type rhythm lick to introduce a song or support a verse. Imagine playing this and singing at the same time. Although each bar clearly implies the chords, you can also consider these phrases to be based on the pentatonic major scale. Notice how the slides add to the fluid feel, and how the same fingering can be used on either the bottom string or the fifth string.

In the right musical context, this can be an interesting alternative to just strumming the chords.

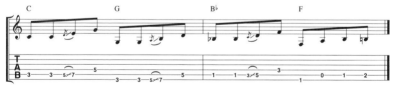

Hendrix-Style Broken Chords

This next example is based on Hendrix's much-admired use of broken-chord accompaniment. It sounds complicated when you hear it, but the technique is actually fairly easy to master. Gene's Steve Mason is another guitarist who uses it.

The trick to playing broken-chord accompaniments is to find a bar chord that can be held down with one finger. This often means playing only three or four strings that give you the essential chord tones. You then use a finger to hammer-on and/or pull-off notes that don't belong in the chord. This produces tension-and-release patterns which can be very expressive.

Play a fifth-fret bar chord, then use the third finger to hammer on successive strings to produce a rising/falling pattern. Try pulling-off as well.

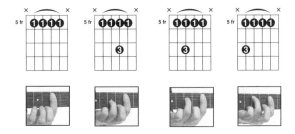

It is also possible to reverse this. Using slightly different fingerings, the extra note(s) end up under the bar so that the hammer-on actually completes the chord and removes the tension.

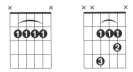

The example below illustrates how this technique might be used in a gentle ballad. Play this one very slowly.

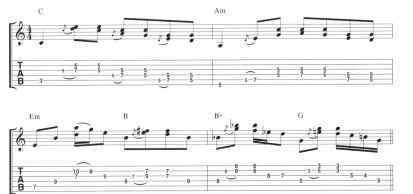

How to Start a Blues Solo

Here's a classic set of blues lead licks for the first four bars of a twelve-bar blues in A.

Unison Bends

Check out the unison bend effect which happens in every bar—D is bent to E and then an E is hit right after it. Hold the top two notes down with your first finger as partial bar and use your third finger to bend the string.

These phrases can be played in any order and in any key—just move them up or down the fretboard as required.

The root note (A) is on the top string at the fifth fret in the first bar. If you wanted to play these phrases in C, you would move that note to the eighth fret and play the same fingerings in that position.

Knopfler-Style Rhythm

Most of the unique guitar sound on Dire Straits' "Sultans of Swing" album came from Mark Knopfler's distinctive picking style. Using a thumb and two fingers to pluck the strings, and resting the third and little fingers on the guitar body, makes it easy to play triads.

Try this interesting picking technique as you play the example below.

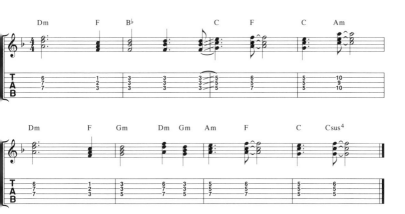

You'll find that playing with your fingers, rather than a pick, opens up many more possibilities of tone and articulation. Try striking the strings with your fingertips—or catching a little bit of nail as you pick. Similarly, where you pick the string can change the sound considerably. Listen to the change in sound as you pick near the bridge, or right up by the fingerboard.

More Blues Licks

The greatest amount of chord movement in a twelve-bar blues occurs in the last four bars. This is called the turnaround because it leads from the end of one twelve-bar sequence back to the beginning of another. Here's a neat phrase that you can just move around as the chords change.

Notice the E at fret 9 in bar 1. That's the root note of the chord over which you're playing. Use that note to locate the phrase somewhere else on the neck if you want to play in a different key.

A twelve-bar blues in G would have a D chord in bar 9, so you would locate that note at fret 7. In fact, this is what happens in bar 2 of this example: everything would move down two frets.

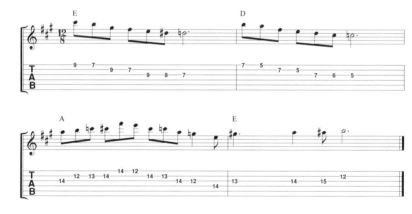

Quick-Change Blues

In blues there is a twelve-bar form known as the *quick-change*. A standard blues has four bars of the key chord with the first change coming in bar 5.

A quick-change blues changes chord in bar 2 and then returns to the key chord in bar 3.

The following simple trick enables you to exploit this when soloing. If you play the first bar on the A pentatonic minor scale at the fifth fret simply move the pattern up two frets in bar 2. You will be on a D pentatonic major scale, which will make a pleasing and highly professional-sounding contrast for that bar (instead of staying with the more predictable A pentatonic minor). The same two-frets-up trick will work in any other bar where there is a D (for example in bars 5, 6, and 10).

Writing Songs

Many guitarists would like to write songs, but they don't necessarily know which chords work best together. There is a simple formula for working this out. Let's pick a guitar friendly key: C major.

The notes of C major are: C D E F G A B C. They are separated by a pattern of intervals: whole step, whole step, half step, whole step, whole step, whole step, half step (in frets: 2 2 1 2 2 2 1). The chords of C major are formed from these notes and follow a fixed sequence: major, minor, minor, major, major, minor, diminished.

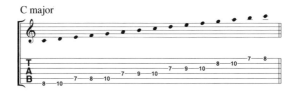

The chords that sound best together in C major are C, Dm, Em, F, G, and Am. The seventh chord, B diminished, can be ignored as it is not often used. We get an acceptable substitute by flatting the seventh note from B to B♭ and turning it into a B♭ major chord. Here are the chords formed from the C major scale.

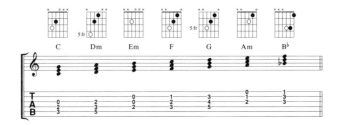

Style Ideas

Here are the same chords for other guitar-friendly keys:

F Major

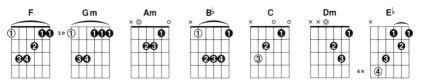

G Major

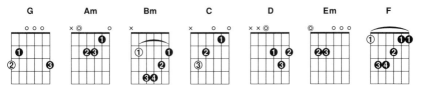

D Major

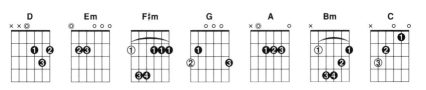

Choose any key and you are free to combine the seven chords in any way you like. Many famous songs use only three or four of the seven!